EVANSTON PUBLIC LIBRARY
1703 ORRINGTON AVENUE
EVANSTON, ILLINOIS 60201

Incredible True Adventures

THE RACE TO THE SOUTH POLE

By Ryan Nagelhout

Gareth Stevens
PUBLISHING

Please visit our website, www.garethstevens.com. For a free color catalog of all our high-quality books, call toll free 1-800-542-2595 or fax 1-877-542-2596.

Library of Congress Cataloging-in-Publication Data

Nagelhout, Ryan.
The race to the South Pole / by Ryan Nagelhout.
p. cm. — (Incredible true adventures)
Includes index.
ISBN 978-1-4824-2042-5 (pbk.)
ISBN 978-1-4824-2041-8 (6-pack)
ISBN 978-1-4824-2043-2 (library binding)
1. Amundsen, Roald, — 1872-1928 — Travel — Juvenile literature. 2. Scott, Robert Falcon, — 1868-1912 — Travel — Juvenile literature. 3.Shackleton, Ernest Henry, — Sir, — 1874-1922 — Juvenile literature.
4. Antarctica — Discovery and exploration — Juvenile literature. 5. South Pole — Discovery and exploration — Juvenile literature. I. Nagelhout, Ryan. II. Title.
G850 1912.A48 N34 2015
919.8—d23

First Edition

Published in 2015 by
Gareth Stevens Publishing
111 East 14th Street, Suite 349
New York, NY 10003

Copyright © 2015 Gareth Stevens Publishing

Designer: Andrea Davison-Bartolotta
Editor: Kristen Rajczak

Photo credits: Cover, pp. 1, 28-29 Elaine Hood/National Science Foundation; p. 4 leonello calvetti/Shutterstock.com; p. 5 Denis Burdin/Shutterstock.com; p. 6 Rainer Lesniewski/Shutterstock.com; p. 7 df028/Shutterstock.com; p. 8 Mogens Trolle/Shutterstock.com; p. 9 (main) Georgios Kollidas/Shutterstock.com; p. 9 (inset) Universal History Archive/UIG/Getty Images; p. 10 The Print Collection/Hulton Archive/Getty Images; p. 11 Lokal_Profil/Wikimedia Commons; pp. 13 (inset), 27 Popperfoto/Getty Images; p. 13 (main) Hulton Archive/Getty Images; pp. 14-15 The Print Collector/Hulton Archive/Getty Images; p. 15 (inset) NYPL/Science Source/Photo Researchers/Getty Images; p. 16 Herbert Ponting/Scott Polar Research Institute, University of Cambridge/Hulton Archive/Getty Images; p. 17 Shakki/Wikimedia Commons; p. 18 Nasjonalbiblioteket/Wikimedia Commons; p. 19 Photo12/UIG/Getty Images; p. 20 Lawrence Oates/Wikimedia Commons; p. 21 Captain Robert Falcon Scott/Popperfoto/Getty Images; p. 22 English School/The Bridgeman Art Library/Getty Images; p. 23 Time Life Pictures/Mansell/The LIFE Picture Collection/Getty Images; p. 24 Dorling Kindersley/Thinkstock; p. 25 General Photographic Agency/Hulton Archive/Getty Images; p. 26 Peter Macdiarmid/Getty Images News/Getty Images; p. 28 (inset) DEA/G. Dagli Orti/De Agostini Picture Library/Getty Images.

All rights reserved. No part of this book may be reproduced in any form without permission in writing from the publisher, except by a reviewer.

Printed in the United States of America

CPSIA compliance information: Batch #CW15GS: For further information contact Gareth Stevens, New York, New York at 1-800-542-2595.

Contents

The Great Race	4
Looking South	6
Finding Antarctica	8
Funding Early Expeditions	10
Discovery	12
"A Live Donkey"	14
Terra Nova and *Fram*	16
Framheim and False Start	18
Scott Sets Off	20
Different Men, Different Expeditions	22
Polheim	24
11 Miles Away	26
Polar Heroes	28
Glossary	30
For More Information	31
Index	32

Words in the glossary appear in **bold** type the first time they are used in the text.

The Great Race

Discovering new places on Earth has tested the will of many explorers who have set out, hoping for adventure and glory. Sighting unmapped continents and islands provided an overwhelming sense of pride to those who made the journey.

However, these discoveries were the results of months at sea and often dangerous voyages. And after hundreds of years, the unexplored parts of Earth became fewer. So, explorers turned to the coldest parts of the planet for glory. Early in the 20th century, two men claimed discovery of the North Pole. The last part of unexplored Earth was to the south on Antarctica. Who would reach the South Pole first?

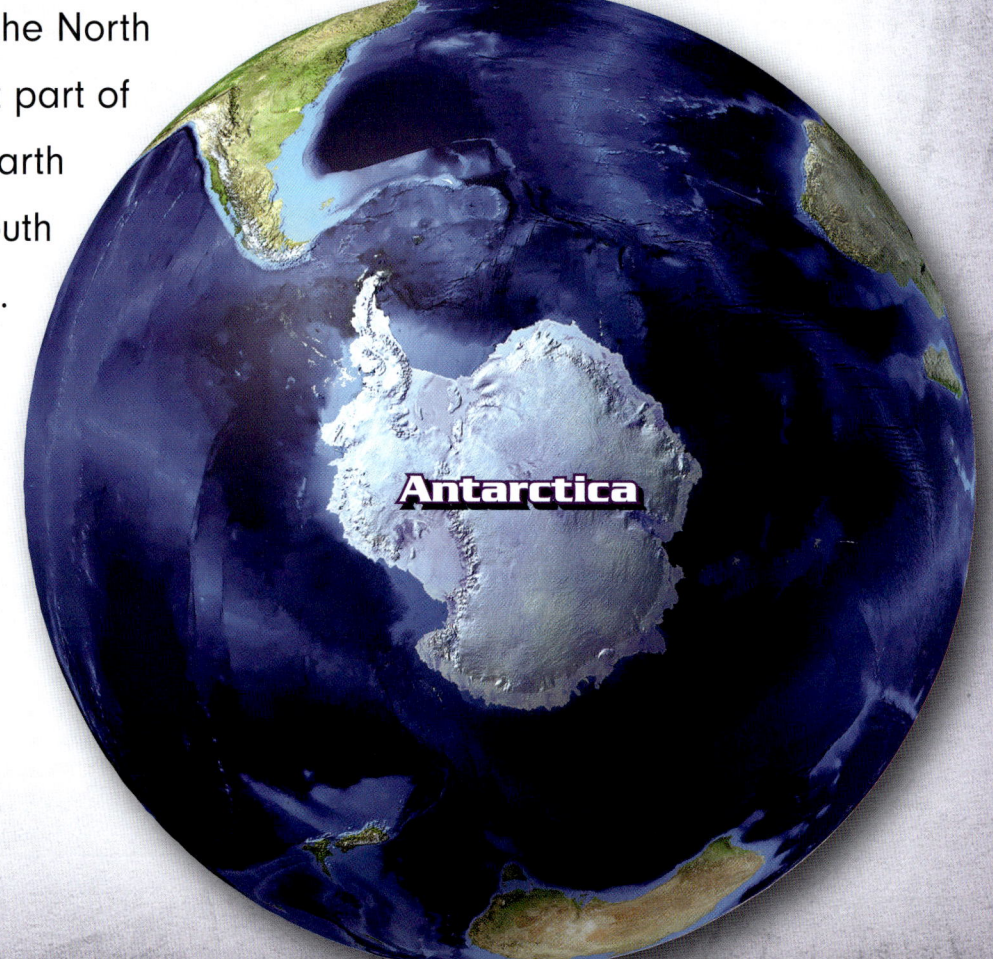

By 1909, the South Pole was one of the few places on Earth no one had reached yet.

Who Claimed the North?

In 1909, two Americans claimed to have reached the North Pole. Frederick Cook claimed he reached the pole in April 1908, while Robert E. Peary said he found it a year later. Cook's claim wasn't confirmed, but it's likely true. Peary's claim is less certain. Even when explorers reach the North Pole, it's hard to mark the spot as the ice there is always moving!

Looking South

Unlike the North Pole's constantly shifting ice, the South Pole is located on the continent of Antarctica. With an average elevation of 7,546 feet (2,300 m), Antarctica is the highest continent on the planet. Covered in layers of ice with tall mountain peaks in the west, Antarctica is a bit bigger than Australia. It's also very dry and is the largest desert in the world.

Antarctica is the coldest place on the planet. The coldest temperature ever recorded there was −135.8°F (−93.2°C)! Nonetheless, some animals have found a way to live there. Seals, penguins, and many kinds of fish make their home on and around the Antarctic coasts.

Pole Position

There are different points on the map scientists consider the "South Pole." The exact bottom of Earth is called the **geographic** South Pole. This is where lines of **longitude** meet on a globe. The "magnetic" South Pole, which can be found using a compass, is actually located off the coast of Antarctica. The first explorers were generally looking for the geographic South Pole.

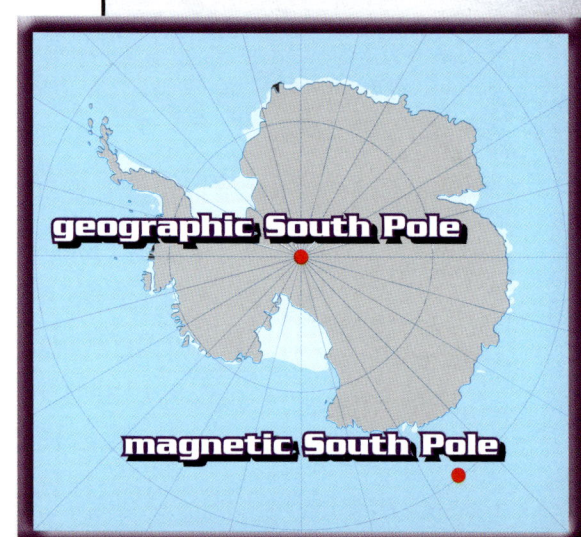

Temperatures on Antarctica usually range from –40° to –94°F (–40° to –70°C).

Finding Antarctica

Many explorers thought a large continent existed at the bottom of Earth, but the **extreme** conditions at such high **latitudes** kept people away for a long time. Captain James Cook and his crew got very close to Antarctica between 1772 and 1775. The continent itself wasn't officially sighted until 1820.

Reaching the South Pole wouldn't happen for almost another century. Even traveling through the flatter eastern side of Antarctica, it would be no easy task. Once discovery of the North Pole was claimed, many explorers began planning to reach the South Pole. The race was on to get to the most **remote** place left on Earth.

Whale and Seal Hunting

One reason many people fought the extreme cold of the Antarctic Circle was in search of whales and seals, which were hunted to make oil. Sealskins, or pelts, were also made into clothing. Hunters kept sailing farther south to find new places to hunt, travels that would help explorers find Antarctica.

Captain James Cook and his crew were the first to sail across the Antarctic Circle, a line of latitude in the Southern **Hemisphere**. They also visited present-day New Zealand.

Funding Early Expeditions

Americans were the first to claim discovery of the North Pole, but many different nations paid for expeditions to the South Pole. Great Britain and Norway made the most famous **polar** expeditions, but Japan, Germany, Sweden, France, and Belgium also funded explorers' trips to Antarctica early in the 20th century.

Each nation funding expeditions hoped explorers would claim the pole for their country as well as learn more about life on Antarctica. For explorers, being the first to reach the South Pole would mean fame and fortune. Planting their nation's flag at the pole first could be the highlight of their life.

French explorer Jean-Baptiste Charcot set off on his first Antarctic expedition in 1903. He charted some of the Antarctic Archipelago, a group of islands off the Antarctic Peninsula.

Who Owns Antarctica?

Many countries claim ownership of land on Antarctica. In 1959, 12 countries that had scientists working in Antarctica signed a written agreement called the Antarctic Treaty. Today, 50 different nations have signed the treaty, which says the continent will be used for "peaceful purposes only." Seven countries—Argentina, Australia, Chile, France, New Zealand, Norway, and the United Kingdom—have territorial claims, which sometimes overlap.

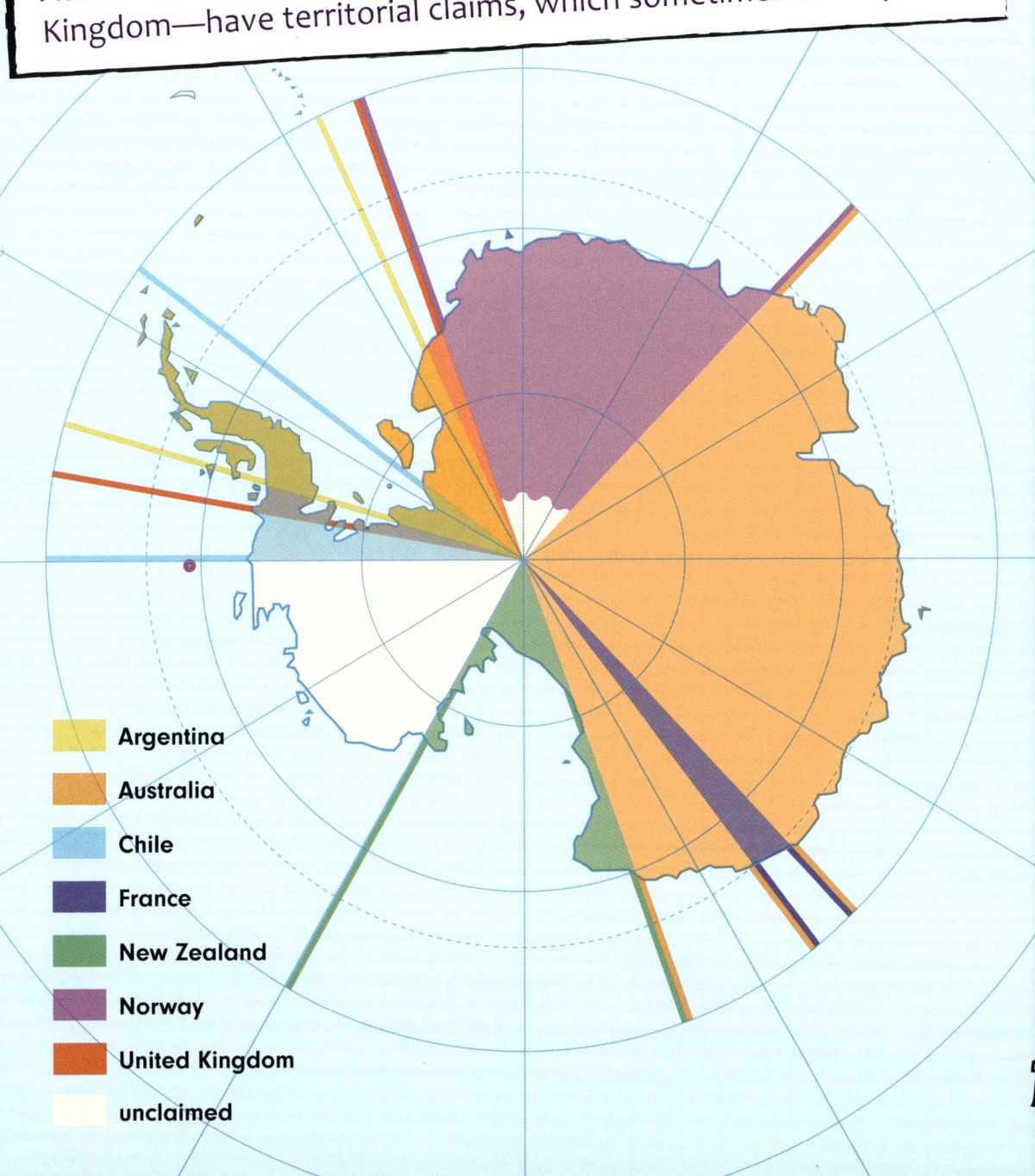

- Argentina
- Australia
- Chile
- France
- New Zealand
- Norway
- United Kingdom
- unclaimed

Discovery

The race to the South Pole truly started in 1900, when Norwegian explorer Carsten Borchgrevink came less than 700 miles (1,127 km) from it while studying Antarctica. In 1901, Robert Falcon Scott set out on a British expedition to the South Pole.

Called the *Discovery* expedition, Scott's was one of the first expeditions with the specific purpose of reaching the South Pole. They also did some scientific experiments on the frozen continent. Scott and two other men—Dr. Edward Wilson and Ernest Shackleton—came within 410 miles (660 km) of the pole. The expedition took 2 years and Shackleton nearly died, but Scott quickly began planning a return trip.

Benefactor

Sir Clements Markham, president of the Royal Geographical Society in England, was the man who pushed for funding of the Discovery expedition. He had an interest in the polar regions after taking part in a search for the bodies of Sir John Franklin and his crew, who died in the Arctic in the 1840s. Making it back home alive was often the hardest part of any polar expedition.

Ernest Shackleton, Robert Falcon Scott, and Edward Wilson

The *Discovery* expedition was named after the RRS *Discovery*, which carried Scott and his crew to Antarctica in 1901.

"A Live Donkey"

After returning to England, Shackleton prepared to make his own trip to Antarctica. He got a ship, *Nimrod*, and prepared a crew and supplies to set sail from England in 1907. After establishing base camp at Cape Royds in McMurdo Sound, Shackleton headed toward the pole.

None of the three trips Shackleton took to the Antarctic went as planned.

The expedition got within 97 miles (156 km) of the South Pole in January 1909. Shackleton knew he couldn't get any closer without risking death in the terrible cold. He and his crew turned back for camp.

After not reaching the pole, Shackleton said just one thing about it to his wife, Emily: "A live donkey is better than a dead lion, isn't it?"

Endurance

Shackleton never reached the South Pole, but he continued exploring the Antarctic. In 1914, he set out on *Endurance* for Antarctica again. The ship got stuck in the ice, however, and the crew was stranded! After a few months, Shackleton led a small group in a lifeboat to a whaling station 16 days away. Not one crewmember died.

Ernest Shackleton

Terra Nova and Fram

Shackleton's failure inspired a number of explorers to make a push for the South Pole. This set up the final race between Scott's second expedition, called *Terra Nova*, and the *Fram* expedition led by Norwegian explorer Roald Amundsen.

Scott's second trip to Antarctica was to follow the same path as Shackleton's *Nimrod* expedition. He and his team set up base camp on Ross Island. Amundsen's *Fram* expedition would take a new route to the pole that was further west on the Ross Ice Shelf. Amundsen set up his base camp at the Bay of Whales, about 400 miles (644 km) from Scott's camp.

Planning in Secret

Amundsen was originally planning an expedition to the North Pole. When he found out that Robert Peary had claimed to reach it first, he changed his mind. "I decided on my change of front—to turn to the right-about, and face to the South," Amundsen wrote. At first, he didn't tell anyone of his change in plans.

members of the *Terra Nova* expedition

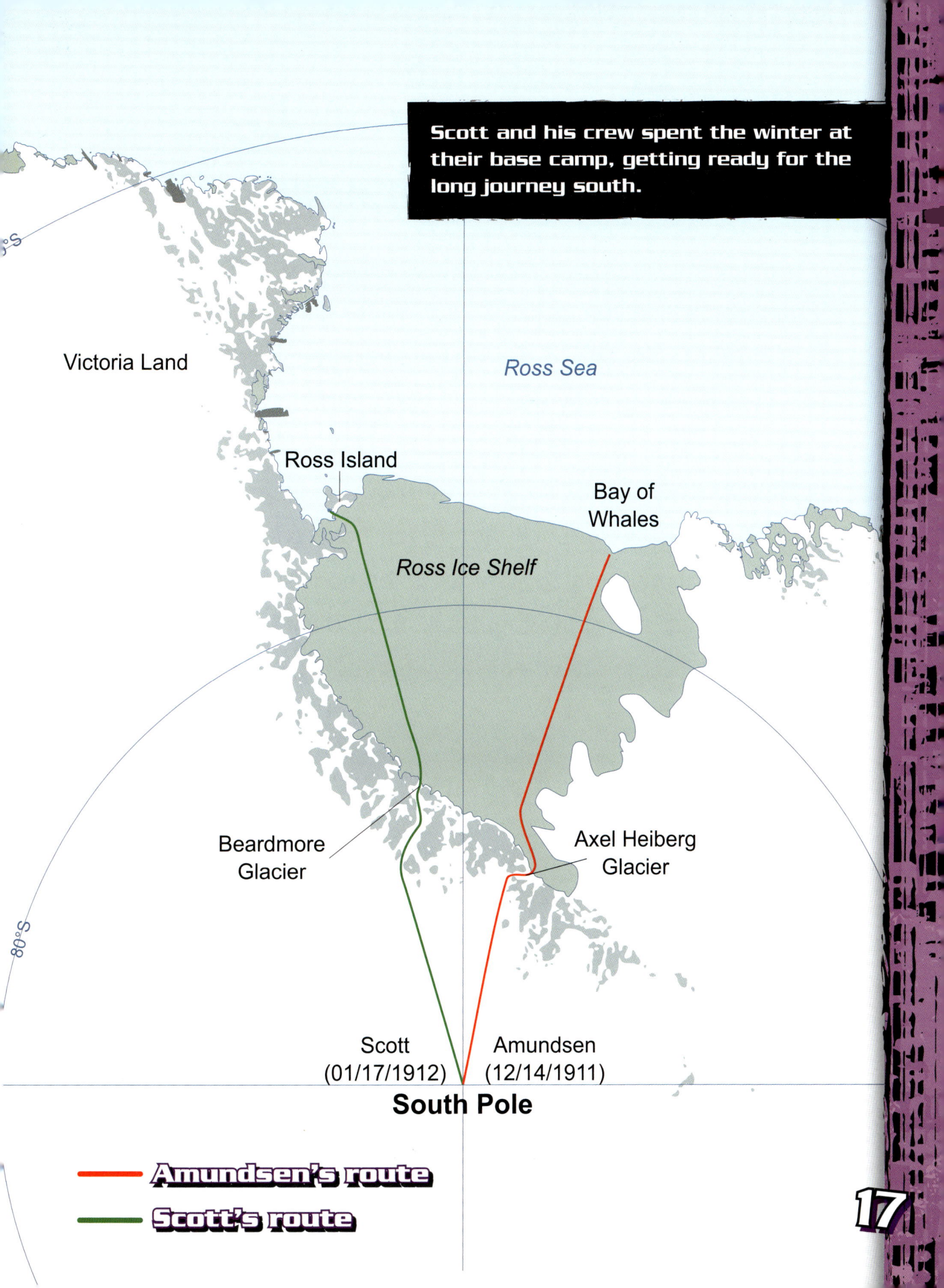

Scott and his crew spent the winter at their base camp, getting ready for the long journey south.

Victoria Land

Ross Sea

Ross Island

Bay of Whales

Ross Ice Shelf

Beardmore Glacier

Axel Heiberg Glacier

Scott (01/17/1912)

Amundsen (12/14/1911)

South Pole

— Amundsen's route
— Scott's route

17

Framheim and False Start

Amundsen set up his base camp, called Framheim ("*Fram* Home"), in January 1911. Known for his thorough planning and attention to **detail**, he carefully considered the tools and **sleds** his crew used. The good planning would pay off for Amundsen and his crew.

Still, Amundsen was so worried about Scott's expedition reaching the South Pole first that he left base camp too early. It was still polar winter in September when he first left Framheim. Four days later, he had to turn back. Amundsen had to leave behind some angry crewmembers when he again started for the pole on October 20.

Framheim

Amundsen quickly found that leaving in September 1911 for the pole was a mistake. "If we are to win the game," Amundsen wrote in his journal, "the pieces must be moved properly; a false move and everything could be lost."

"It's Panic"

Hjalmar Johansen was the most **experienced** explorer on Amundsen's original team. He thought Amundsen made a dangerous mistake when the first explorers had to turn back because of the extremely cold temperatures. "I don't call it an expedition," Johansen said. "It's panic." An angry Amundsen took Johansen off his final crew, taking just five people to the South Pole.

Scott Sets Off

Scott left Ross Island with a large crew, motorized sleds, dogs, and ponies on November 1, 1911, more than a week after Amundsen left Framheim a second time. Scott not only started later, but also planned on completing scientific study along the way, which may have slowed him down.

Scott didn't know the Norwegian explorers were taking a new path to the pole. Neither party knew where their rivals were on the huge, cold continent. Both expeditions believed they'd be able to reach the South Pole, but no one knew who would get there first.

Depots

Both expeditions had set up depots in different spots on their journey ahead of time. Depots were places with food, gear, and other supplies to be used by each party on their return trip back to base camp. Both groups knew getting back home would be the hardest part of the trip.

depot

Scott took ponies on his journey to the South Pole because Shackleton had. However, they weren't well suited to the extreme cold.

Different Men, Different Expeditions

There were many differences between the *Terra Nova* and *Fram* expeditions. They took different routes and had different methods of travel.

Amundsen's men were all great skiers, which helped them move quickly over the ice and snow. Their special sleds of supplies—each weighing 880 pounds (400 kg)—were pulled by 13 dogs apiece. The ponies Scott brought to pull supplies died in the cold, and his team's motor sleds stopped working in the extreme temperatures. He eventually sent his dog teams back to camp, too, so the men had to drag their own sleds along slowly on foot the last leg of the expedition.

Good Eats?

Explorers often ate food called pemmican to survive in the cold. Pemmican is a mixture of dried meat—usually beef, deer, bison, or elk—that is crushed into a powder and mixed with animal fat. Pemmican gave explorers energy and lasted a long time—perfect for the months they spent in the cold.

Being Norwegian was a big help to Amundsen's party. Norway is a cold, snowy country, and many of them had been skiing since childhood, making the trip to the South Pole at least a little easier.

Polheim

On January 17, 1912, Robert Falcon Scott and his party finally arrived at the South Pole. He was nearly 5 weeks too late. Rather than find the most remote place on Earth, Scott found Polheim, the camp Amundsen and his crew had established on December 14, 1911, when they reached the South Pole first.

Amundsen had left a tent, some supplies, and a note for Norway's King Haakon VII on special notebook paper. He also left a note for Scott describing his trip in case something happened to Amundsen on the trip back. Little did he know it would be Scott headed for disaster on the ice.

Back at Framheim

Amundsen and his team arrived back at Framheim early on January 26, 1912. Despite the long and difficult trip, the party was able to leave supplies behind in case Scott needed them. Upon returning to Framheim, Amundsen went right to his cook. "Good morning, my dear Lindstrøm," Amundsen said. "Have you any coffee for us?"

Amundsen's team placed the Norwegian flag at the South Pole to mark their success.

11 Miles Away

Defeated and hungry, Scott turned back for camp, taking Amundsen's letter with him. The *Terra Nova* expedition struggled through mile after mile of ice and snow. Scott's decision to have a fifth member of his crew meant they ran out of supplies faster.

The men were slowly starving and also had **hypothermia** and **scurvy**. On February 17, Edgar Evans died near Beardmore Glacier. A month later, Lawrence Oates left his tent to die in the cold. About 2 weeks later, Scott, Edward Wilson, and Henry Bowers froze to death in their tent. They were just 11 miles (18 km) from one of their depots.

Scott's last journal entry

Sticking It Out

Scott often wrote about the bravery of his crew in his journal until the day he died. "We shall stick it out to the end," Scott wrote, "but we are getting weaker, of course, and the end cannot be far. It seems a pity but I do not think I can write more."

It took 6 months of searching to find the bodies of Scott and his crew.

Polar Heroes

Even in failure and death, Scott and his crew were considered heroes. He had bested Shackleton and missed making history by just a few weeks.

Meanwhile, Amundsen returned to Norway a national hero. Though he stayed just 3 days at the South Pole, his victory in the race to the bottom of Earth made him famous worldwide. In fact, both men died heroes. Scott's life ended on Antarctica, but Amundsen would die in the north in 1928 when his plane crashed into the Arctic Ocean while trying to rescue explorers near the North Pole.

Amundsen's expedition to the North Pole

For those living and working at the Amundsen-Scott South Pole Station, it's dark 6 months of the year!

The South Pole Today

People actually live at the South Pole today! The Amundsen-Scott South Pole Station was built in 1956 and has scientists from around the world living and working there. The station was named after both Amundsen and Scott because both men are celebrated for their race to the most remote place on Earth.

Glossary

detail: a small part

experienced: having skills gained by doing something

extreme: to a very great degree

geographic: having to do with the study of Earth and its features

hemisphere: one half of Earth

hypothermia: dangerously low body temperature caused by cold conditions

latitude: the imaginary lines that run east and west above and below the equator

longitude: the imaginary lines that run north and south to the left and right of the Prime Meridian

polar: having to do with Earth's poles

remote: far removed in place or time

scurvy: a disease caused by a lack of vitamin C

sled: a cart with runners that moves over ice and snow

For More Information

Books

Bodden, Valerie. *To the South Pole.* Mankato, MN: Creative Education, 2011.

Buckley, James. *Who Was Ernest Shackleton?* New York, NY: Grosset & Dunlap, 2013.

Websites

Amundsen's South Pole Expedition
ngm.nationalgeographic.com/2011/09/amundsen/antarctica-video
Watch video of Roald Amundsen getting ready for his trip to the South Pole.

South Pole Station Webcams
usap.gov/videoclipsandmaps/spwebcam.cfm
Watch a live camera feed of life at the South Pole.

Publisher's note to educators and parents: Our editors have carefully reviewed these websites to ensure that they are suitable for students. Many websites change frequently, however, and we cannot guarantee that a site's future contents will continue to meet our high standards of quality and educational value. Be advised that students should be closely supervised whenever they access the Internet.

Index

Amundsen, Roald 16, 18, 19, 20, 22, 23, 24, 25, 26, 28, 29

Amundsen-Scott South Pole Station 29

Antarctic Circle 8, 9

Antarctic Treaty 11

base camp 16, 17, 18, 20

Bay of Whales 16

Borchgravink, Carsten 12

Cook, James 8, 9

depots 20, 26

Discovery expedition 12, 13

Endurance 15

Fram expedition 16, 22

Framheim 18, 20, 24

geographic South Pole 6

Johansen, Hjalmar 19

magnetic South Pole 6

Nimrod 14, 16

North Pole 4, 5, 6, 8, 10, 16, 28

Polheim 24

Ross Island 16, 20

Scott, Robert Falcon 12, 13, 16, 17, 18, 20, 21, 22, 24, 26, 27, 28, 29

Shackleton, Ernest 12, 13, 14, 15, 16, 21, 28

Terra Nova expedition 16, 22, 26

Wilson, Edward 12, 13, 26